The Borrower's Advantage

5 Proven Techniques In Turning
Loans Into Lasting Wealth

Eric Graham

Copyright © 2024 Eric Graham

All Rights Reserved. No part of this publication may be scanned, uploaded, reproduced, stored in a retrieval system or transmitted in any form or by any means: electronic, mechanical, photocopy, recording, or otherwise without the express written permission of the author or publisher except in the case of brief quotations in a book review.

DEDICATION

I dedicate this book to my lovely wife in taking care of the house for me to work on this material.

ACKNOWLEDGEMENT

I am grateful to God Almighty for His leading by His Holy Spirit in helping me put this material together.

I am also grateful for all the individuals who have helped in making this project a reality:

Contents

Dedication

Acknowledgement

Introduction

Developing A Plan to Repay Your Debt

Building Wealth Through Real Estate Financing

Borrowing for Personal Growth

Scaling Businesses with Debt Financing

Maximizing Investments with Margin Loans

Financing Passive Income Streams

Conclusion

Introduction

Borrowing is a game-changer in a society where financial opportunities are generally viewed through the evaluation of risk and return. It's simple to view loans as a burdensome expense that should be avoided at all costs. But what if you could utilize debt as a tool for personal development rather than as a liability?

What if borrowing turned out to be the secret to achieving personal development, business success, and financial independence? Turning loans into a potent wealth-building tactic is precisely what this book is about.

The widespread perception that borrowing is dangerous is frequently the result of a lack of knowledge about how debt functions when used strategically. However, in practice, wealthy and successful people frequently use borrowing to increase their fortune exponentially rather than merely preserve it. When utilized prudently and judiciously, the correct type of debt can increase your profits, open up new options, and help you reach financial independence.

Loans can help you reach your objectives more quickly and efficiently than you may have thought, whether you're trying to invest in real estate, improve your education, expand your business, or generate passive income.

I'll teach you how to use borrowing to your advantage throughout this book. Taking on additional debt for its own sake is not the goal here. Rather, it's about knowing how to strategically use borrowing to your benefit. From real estate investing to business expansion, we'll examine various aspects of borrowing in each chapter and show you how to use loans to boost your financial development while controlling risks and keeping a sound financial balance.

Leverage is a key idea that underpins our strategy, so let's start there before getting into the details. Leverage, to put it simply, is the use of borrowed funds to raise the possible return on an investment. The idea may appear simple, but the interesting part is how it manifests itself in several spheres of life, including business, education, real estate, and passive income. You'll see how leverage loans can transform modest investments into significant opportunities as we go over each chapter.

The Distinctions Between Traditional and Wealth-Based Borrowing

Most people associate borrowing with credit cards, personal loans, and the ongoing stress of debt repayment. However, strategic borrowing is a whole different strategy. Instead of going into debt with little financial benefit, it's about using loans to add value and provide returns.

Consider real estate as an example. Though few have the funds to purchase huge homes outright, many people aspire to own real estate. Here's where mortgages are useful. You can control assets worth far more than you could with just your own funds if you borrow money to buy real estate. The secret is that real estate typically increases in value over time, and with the correct approach, the returns can significantly exceed the mortgage payment. Wealth is created in this way.

In a similar vein, borrowing money to fund personal development and education is a wise move. A more prosperous job and higher earning potential can result from using education loans to obtain a degree or certification. When you take out a loan to continue your education, the return on investment frequently much outweighs the original loan amount.

Entrepreneurs can scale their businesses faster by using loans to finance operations, expansion, or innovation than they could with just their own savings. Businesses can expand quickly thanks to debt, which opens up previously unattainable profit-making prospects. Additionally, if handled properly, margin loans give investors the opportunity to increase their returns.

However, borrowing has more power than that. The use of debt to support passive income streams— businesses or assets that produce steady income with little active participation—is also covered in this book. You can build long-term revenue streams and achieve financial independence by taking out loans to finance these endeavors.

In Chapter 1, *Building Wealth Through Real Estate Financing*, we'll explore how leveraging mortgages can help you get into real estate, control larger assets with less upfront capital, and amplify your wealth. The chapter will teach you how to evaluate properties, choose financing options, and manage the risks involved in property investments.

Chapter 2, *The Power of Borrowing for Personal Growth*, focuses on how educational loans can propel your career. We'll dive into how borrowing for education can lead to higher earning potential and greater career satisfaction, and we'll provide strategies for managing debt while ensuring a solid return on investment.

Chapter 3, *Scaling Businesses with Debt Financing*, shows how borrowing can be the key to scaling your business. Whether you're a startup or an established business, we'll walk through how loans can fund growth, help you expand operations, and maintain financial health while scaling your business.

In Chapter 4, *Maximizing Investments with Margin Loans*, we'll examine the mechanics of margin loans and how they can be used to amplify returns on investments. This chapter will also explore the risks involved and provide strategies for managing debt and building a balanced, diversified portfolio.

Finally, Chapter 5, *Financing Passive Income Streams*, will teach you how to use loans to fund passive income ventures, from real estate to e-commerce. You'll learn how to build, scale, and automate income streams that provide long-term wealth with minimal ongoing effort.

As you read through each chapter, you'll begin to see how loans—far from being a source of stress—can become a strategic tool that accelerates your wealth-building efforts. But remember, as with any financial strategy, the key is discipline. Understand the risks, know how to manage debt, and be strategic about where and how you borrow.

The path to financial freedom doesn't have to be slow and painstaking. By using borrowing as a lever, you can accelerate your progress and achieve your financial goals faster than you might have thought possible. It's time to stop avoiding debt and start using it to create the life you want.

Let's dive in and unlock the power of borrowing for wealth-building.

Chapter 1

Developing A Plan to Repay Your Debt

"The secret of getting ahead is getting started." — Mark Twain

One of the most important concepts to grasp when using loans to build wealth is that borrowed funds ought to be utilized to produce returns greater than the expense of borrowing. The objective is to make sure that the investments you make with borrowed money generate earnings that not only pay off the loan balance but also help you build wealth over the long run, rather than just taking on debt. This method necessitates a methodical approach, meticulous preparation, and a firm grasp of how various loan kinds operate.

When you borrow money for a specific purpose, such as funding a business initiative, paying for school, or investing in real estate, you are demonstrating that your decision is in line with your long-term financial objectives. It is about borrowing for investments rather than for consumption.

For instance, you can create passive income while the property's value increases by taking out a mortgage to purchase a rental property. Over time, this kind of borrowing may yield profits that much outweigh the interest payments. You are effectively letting other people's money work for you when you utilize borrowed money to invest in assets that generate income. If done properly, this can be a very potent tool.

However, it is crucial to pay attention to cash flow to make sure the loan doesn't become a financial burden. The money that comes into and goes out of your pockets is referred to as cash flow, and when employing borrowed funds, a positive cash flow is essential to financial success.

If you take out a loan to purchase a property, for example, the rental income should ideally be greater than your monthly costs and mortgage payments, giving you additional money. Stress and financial strain may result if your investment is not producing enough cash flow to comfortably satisfy your loan obligations. Make sure the investment or property you're funding is thoroughly investigated and anticipated to produce consistent cash flow to prevent this.

Selecting loans with acceptable terms is just as important as paying attention to cash flow. Maintaining cash flow while repaying the debt is made easier by a low interest rate, which can drastically lower the loan's overall cost over time.

Examine interest rates, repayment plans, and the total cost of the loan before accepting any. If at all feasible, seek out solutions that include flexible repayment schedules so that, when your financial circumstances improve, you can pay off the loan sooner. In order to continue making repayments even in difficult financial times, it's also critical to establish an emergency fund to meet unforeseen costs.

Lastly, having a clear and practical payback plan is essential to managing debt payments without creating excessive stress. You may keep on track by automating payments, allocating a particular percentage of your income for loan repayment, and maintaining a strict budget.

Keep in mind that although debt can be an effective instrument for generating wealth, it must be managed carefully and strategically to avoid becoming a financial burden.

Selecting Appropriate Loan Conditions to Promote Simpler Repayment

The manageability of your debt payments is greatly influenced by the conditions of your loan. Selecting the appropriate loan arrangement is essential to guaranteeing that you can make the most of borrowed money without being burdened with excessive repayment obligations. Your financial status may be significantly impacted by the interest rates, repayment plans, and flexibility of the various loan kinds.

Selecting a fixed or variable interest rate is one of the first choices you must make when selecting a loan. A fixed-rate loan offers stability and predictability by locking in an interest rate for the term of the loan. If you want to minimize the risk of rising interest rates and want regularity in your monthly payments, this is a great option.

A variable-rate loan, on the other hand, varies according to market conditions, which may lead to higher payments when interest rates rise but also lower payments when rates are low. You run the danger of having to make larger payments if interest rates rise, even if a variable-rate loan can save you money in the near run. Therefore, before deciding between these two loan options, it's critical to evaluate your financial stability and risk tolerance.

The payback time is another factor to take into account when choosing a loan. Higher monthly payments are usually associated with shorter loan terms, but they enable you to pay off the debt faster, thus saving you money on interest. Conversely, longer loan terms result in cheaper monthly payments, but over the course of the loan, you will pay more interest.

A longer-term loan can be more appropriate if you have a steady source of income and would rather make smaller monthly payments to free up funds for other investments or spending. A shorter-term loan might be a better choice, though, if you value paying off your debt as soon as possible and lowering interest expenses.

Another alternative available to borrowers to enhance loan terms and make repayment simpler is refinancing. Refinancing is the process of taking out a new loan with better terms, like a longer repayment period or a cheaper interest rate, to pay off an existing one. This can provide you greater financial flexibility, decrease the total cost of the loan, and lower monthly payments.

Refinancing isn't always the best course of action, though, so it's crucial to balance the possible savings against the expenditures. Refinancing can be a wise choice to lessen the weight of debt if interest rates have dropped or if your credit score has increased since you initially obtained the loan.

Another tactic that can make repayments easier is debt consolidation. You can simplify your payments, lower interest rates, and lengthen the repayment period by combining several loans into one, which will make debt management simpler.

Consolidating debt should be done carefully, though, as it occasionally results in a longer payback period and more interest over time. It's critical to thoroughly assess whether consolidation actually improves your financial status and matches with your long-term financial objectives.

In the end, knowing your financial status and long-term goals is crucial to choosing the best loan conditions. It's important to make sure that the conditions of your loan match your capacity to repay without jeopardizing your financial security, regardless of whether you decide on a fixed or variable rate, short- or long-term loan, or refinance. The repayment process can be made much easier with the correct loan terms, enabling you to keep accumulating wealth and reaching your financial objectives.

Creating a Strategic Plan for Paying Off Debt to Increase Wealth

A well-thought-out debt repayment plan is essential to efficiently manage borrowed money while carrying on with investments and wealth accumulation. Debt repayment can become daunting if you don't have a clear strategy in place, and you could find it difficult to strike a balance between your financial commitments and your aspirations to accumulate money. You can make sure that your loan repayments don't conflict with your financial goals or investing strategy by developing a structured debt repayment plan.

The debt snowball method is one efficient way to handle debt payments. This tactic is making minimum payments on larger debts while concentrating on paying off the smaller obligation first. You pay off the smallest debt first, then the next smallest, and so on.

As you watch your obligations go away one by one, this method gives you drive and a sense of accomplishment. Additionally, it enables you to concentrate on smaller, easier-to-manage sums, which can lessen the burden of debt repayment. The debt snowball approach might not always be the most economical, particularly if you have high-interest debt, even though it might be psychologically satisfying.

As an alternative, the debt avalanche strategy focuses on paying off high-interest debt ahead of lower-interest debt while making minimum payments on the latter. By gradually lowering the interest you pay, this strategy lowers the total cost of borrowing. You may pay off your debt faster and have more money to invest in assets that will increase your wealth by giving high-interest loans priority. Although the debt avalanche method is a more cost-effective tactic, some borrowers may become less motivated because it may take longer to see results.

Along with employing these debt-payback techniques, it's critical to create a sensible budget that includes money for both debt repayment and investments that increase wealth. You can make sure you're managing debt and continuing to accumulate money by making a budget that accounts for both your monthly loan payments and your investment contributions.

This well-rounded strategy is necessary for sustained financial success. To make sure that your financial priorities align with your objectives, it's also critical to periodically review your budget.

Consistency is another essential element of a planned debt repayment plan. You can keep on track and never miss a payment by setting up automated debt repayment. By doing this, you can save needless stress, late penalties, and harm to your credit score.

At the same time, you can steadily increase your wealth by automating investments in return-producing assets. Consistency in debt repayment and wealth-building endeavors is essential, regardless of whether you invest in stocks, real estate, or other assets that provide income.

You may make sure that your borrowed money is utilized to its maximum potential and enable you to accumulate wealth while efficiently managing debt by creating a smart debt repayment plan that complements your financial objectives. Debt repayment can be made a reasonable procedure that contributes to your long-term financial success with careful preparation, perseverance, and dedication.

Chapter 2

Building Wealth Through Real Estate Financing

"The best time to plant a tree was 20 years ago. The second best time is now." — *Chinese Proverb*

Leveraging Mortgages to Maximize Real Estate Investments

The ability to leverage mortgages is one of the most important tools for success in real estate investing. In essence, a mortgage is a loan that enables investors to buy a property with relatively little of its entire worth coming from their own funds.

The loan covers the remaining and is paid back over time with interest. With the help of this leverage, investors are able to manage larger properties than they could if they only used their personal funds. Depending on the down payment and loan conditions, an investor may be able to purchase a $300,000 property with a mortgage and only need to spend $60,000 or less up front. Compared to having to own houses outright, this enables more varied investment portfolios and faster wealth growth.

Leverage plays a critical part in accumulating wealth in real estate. Since real estate usually increases in value over time, your chances of making money increase with the size of the property you can manage. Although leverage magnifies both profits and losses, it can greatly increase return on investment when applied wisely.

For instance, if an investor purchases a $300,000 home with a mortgage and it increases in value by 5% over the course of a year, the investor will have made $15,000. But compared to other investment types, the return on the investor's initial investment of $60,000 is a considerably greater 25%, which is an impressive return.

Real estate is a significant instrument for accumulating wealth since rental properties also have the ability to generate monthly income, which can increase the total return.

For real estate investors who employ leverage, it is essential to comprehend how debt improves returns on investment. The idea that debt enables the investor to utilize other people's money—the bank's—to create wealth and income is the foundation of the notion that debt may be used to develop riches.

For instance, while renting out a property, the renter effectively pays off the investor's mortgage. The investor gains a profitable asset as the property's value increases and the loan balance falls over time. The secret to success is making sure that rental income is more than maintenance, taxes, and mortgage payments. This will result in a positive cash flow. When set up correctly, this strategy enables the investor to increase their wealth and equity in the property at the same time.

The possibility of "equity buildup," or the gradual growth in the investor's ownership stake in the property as the mortgage sum is paid off, is also made possible by leverage. The investor's equity in the property increases as a percentage of each mortgage payment is applied to the loan principal.

Over time, this equity and the property's value growth can lead to a sizable increase in wealth. Investors can further increase their returns by maximizing their profitability by utilizing low-interest rates, which will result in lower interest payments over the loan's duration.

Finding Lucrative Properties and Funding Sources

Finding properties that can yield profits is the first stage in a successful real estate investment strategy. Understanding the elements that go into making a successful investment is crucial. Analyzing a possible property's location is one of the most crucial aspects in the evaluation process.

Long-term investments in properties in desirable communities are safer since their value tends to increase more steadily over time. Additionally, a property's appeal to potential tenants or buyers may be enhanced by its close proximity to facilities like parks, schools, public transportation, and shopping malls.

Assessing the potential for property value rise also requires an understanding of local market patterns, such as supply and demand dynamics.

Estimating the possible rental income and contrasting it with the expenses of property ownership is a crucial phase in the appraisal process. This covers maintenance, repairs, insurance, property taxes, and mortgage payments. Making sure that rental income will cover all costs and allow space for profit is the aim. The 1% rule, which stipulates that the monthly rent must equal at least 1% of the property's purchase price, is a popular guideline among real estate investors.

This is a decent place to start when determining if a property is worth considering, but it is not a guarantee of profitability. By estimating projected revenue and expenses over time, tools such as cash flow analysis spreadsheets can assist investors in more correctly assessing possible properties.

A crucial choice that can impact an investment's overall profitability is selecting the appropriate mortgage structure for different kinds of real estate investments. There are several types of mortgages, each with unique benefits and risks.

For instance, a fixed-rate mortgage enables the investor to budget for regular payments over time and offers predictable payments, making it a good choice for long-term investments. As an alternative, investors who intend to sell or refinance before the rate changes may find that adjustable-rate mortgages (ARMs) provide lower starting interest rates. However, because interest rates can change and impact future payments, ARMs can create anxiety. Investors should think about whether a 15-, 20-, or 30-year loan duration is ideal for their investment strategy in addition to the mortgage structure.

In real estate investing, obtaining advantageous financing arrangements is essential to optimizing earnings and lowering risks. The interest rate is a crucial factor that can have a big impact on the mortgage's total cost.

Cash flow will be improved by a reduced interest rate since it will lead to smaller monthly payments and less interest paid overall. Investors should also concentrate on obtaining advantageous loan-to-value (LTV) ratios. Although this can vary according on the lender and loan type, most lenders ask a down payment of at least 20% for investment properties.

For both the lender and the investor, the lower the LTV, the smaller the risk. To identify the best funding choices for their investment strategy, investors should also investigate a variety of lending sources, such as conventional banks, credit unions, and alternative lenders like hard-money or private lenders.

Risk Control in Finance for Real Estate

Like any other investment, real estate has hazards that need to be properly controlled. Market volatility is one of the main hazards associated with real estate investments. Cycles of boom and bust can occur in the real estate market, and a number of reasons, including local market circumstances, interest rate increases, and economic downturns, can cause property values to drop.

Investors may become "underwater" on their loans—that is, owe more on the mortgage than the property is worth—when property values decline. Financial troubles may result from this, particularly if the investor is unable to refinance or sell the home. Diversifying the real estate portfolio by making investments in a range of property kinds and locations is crucial to reducing this risk. This makes it less likely that a decline in one market will totally destroy an investor's whole holdings.

Another big risk associated with real estate investing is tenant problems. A rental property's profitability depends heavily on its rental income, and any vacancy or non-payment of rent can have a negative effect on cash flow.

To reduce the chance of late payments or property damage, it is crucial to thoroughly research potential renters and create explicit rental agreements. Maintaining financial stability in real estate investments also requires setting up an emergency fund to cover vacancies, repairs, and unforeseen expenses.

In order to reduce the risks associated with maintenance problems and tenant turnover, investors could also think about hiring property management services to take care of the daily duties of overseeing tenants.

In order to control risks in real estate financing, diversification and due diligence are essential. Before making a purchase, due diligence is doing extensive research on a property, including assessing the neighborhood, the local market, and the property's condition.

It also entails evaluating the investment's financial factors, including possible rental income, costs, and financing alternatives. Diversification can assist lower a portfolio's overall risk, both inside the real estate market and across various asset classes.

To reduce the risk of one market segment underperforming, an investor can decide to invest in both residential and commercial properties. Additionally, in the event of regional economic downturns, investing across multiple geographic locations can help distribute risk.

Maintaining the viability of real estate assets over time requires careful management of cash flow and long-term profitability. To pay for operating costs and make mortgage payments on schedule, a positive cash flow must be maintained. Investors may have to take out loans or use their own funds to keep afloat if rental income is insufficient to pay for expenses.

Important cash flow management techniques include monitoring each property's financial performance on a regular basis, modifying rentals, and controlling operating expenses. Rental revenue, cost-effective property management, and property appreciation can all lead to long-term profitability.

In order to improve overall returns and offset expenses, investors should also take into account the possibility of tax deductions and depreciation.

Thought Room

Are you willing to take the leap into real estate investing, or do the risks seem overwhelming?

Have you thought about how leveraging loans can accelerate your wealth-building process?

What steps can you take today to identify a profitable property to invest in?

Chapter 3
Borrowing for Personal Growth

"An investment in knowledge pays the best interest."
— *Benjamin Franklin*

Educational Loans: Investing in Human Capital

Many people believe that taking out a loan to pay for school is essential to raising earning potential and is the secret to long-term success and financial stability. People are investing in their most valuable asset—human capital—when they take out loans to pay for specialized training or higher education.

Based on economic theory, this idea contends that people's acquired skills, knowledge, and abilities through education are just as valuable as tangible assets like stocks or real estate. Over time, a higher return on investment (ROI) can result from investing in education because it can lead to professional development, higher-paying positions, and more job stability.

Realizing the long-term financial gains from investing in one's education and training is essential to appreciating the worth of student loans. People can seek professional training, degrees, and certificates that greatly boost their earning potential by taking out loans for their schooling.

Higher educated people typically make more money over the course of their careers, according to a wealth of research. The U.S. Bureau of Labor Statistics estimates that people with a bachelor's degree make about 65% more money each week than someone with just a high school degree.

With higher degrees or specialized certificates, this income potential rises even more, making education a tremendous instrument for gradually increasing wealth.

However, evaluating the return on investment (ROI) of particular degrees, certifications, or professional training programs is essential to getting the most out of an educational loan. Even if a broad college degree could significantly increase one's salary, some subjects pay more than others.

For instance, degrees in the humanities typically yield lower salaries than those in STEM (Science, Technology, Engineering, and Mathematics) professions. Furthermore, without the time and cost of a four-year degree, investing in professional training and certifications can be an affordable method to increase earning potential. Making thoughtful choices about what to study, where to study, and how much debt to take on is essential to making sure that the school loan has a beneficial financial impact.

Beyond the short-term pay boost, investing in knowledge and skills has long-term benefits. Education is a tool for empowerment and personal development. It gives people the self-assurance, problem-solving, and critical thinking skills they need to succeed in a labor market that is changing quickly.

Those who have made an investment in ongoing education are better equipped to adjust, innovate, and maintain their relevance in their careers as new technologies and industries arise.

In addition to increasing their earning potential, people who take out loans to invest in their education also protect their jobs from the unpredictability of a constantly shifting economy.

Using Strategic Borrowing to Open Up Career Paths

Strategic borrowing can be a potent tool in today's economy to open up job chances and boost professional development. People can advance their careers more quickly and access possibilities that might otherwise be unattainable by taking out loans to seek higher education or specialized skills training. This is particularly true in professions where leadership or higher-paying roles need specialized knowledge or advanced certifications.

Loans are a common way for professionals to invest in their professional growth. For instance, people who work in professions like engineering, law, or medicine frequently take out large student loans to finish their studies and obtain the credentials required to practice in those fields.

In a similar vein, those who want to progress in their employment could take out loans to pay for professional certification or specialized training. By making such investments, people can obtain a competitive advantage in the labor market, putting them in a position to advance in their careers and earn more money and prestigious titles.

There are numerous real-world examples of people who have deliberately exploited debt to further their careers. For example, a lot of successful executives and business owners have used school loans to pay for advanced degrees like an MBA, which has given them access to leadership roles or the chance to launch their own businesses.

For instance, Jeff Bezos turned his academic investments into enormous business success by using his Princeton University degree and early professional skills to finally start Amazon. Similar to this, professionals like doctors, lawyers, and others frequently experience a large return on their college loans since their degrees land them well-paying jobs in their industries.

The secret to effectively using loans to further your profession is striking a balance between the increased income from your education or new skills and the repayment procedure. Taking out a loan to fund college necessitates managing debt strategically.

Following graduation or the conclusion of a certification program, people should concentrate on finding better-paying employment and adjusting their payback schedule to reflect their increased income. It is crucial to keep a balanced approach by making sure that loan repayments don't impair the borrower's capacity to invest in additional professional growth or reduce their financial security.

Taking Care of Debt for Financial Stability and Personal Development

A key component of guaranteeing both long-term financial security and personal development is prudent debt management. Although taking out loans to further your school or career can provide significant benefits, it is important to manage your debt carefully to prevent unnecessary financial burden.

In addition to helping people pay off their debts quickly, a well-thought-out debt management plan can allow them to keep making investments in their long-term financial objectives and personal development.

Knowing the long-term effects of borrowing is one of the most important components of efficient debt management. Individuals must account for years of repayment obligations when they take out college loans in their overall financial strategy. For instance, the amount of debt accrued from student loans can have a big influence on a person's capacity to participate in other wealth-building ventures, buy a home, or save for retirement.

Borrowers should think carefully about how much debt they have compared to their income and how long it will take to pay it back. Borrowers who comprehend this relationship are better able to prioritize their finances and make sure that their debt commitments do not overwhelm them.

In order to manage debt and maximize career rewards, repayment techniques are crucial. The "debt snowball" method, which entails paying off smaller bills first and gradually taking on larger ones, is one popular tactic. As an alternative, the "debt avalanche" strategy saves money on interest over time by paying off the loan with the highest interest rate first.

Depending on a person's tastes and financial status, either approach may work well. In order to reduce interest rates and streamline the repayment procedure, borrowers could also think about refinancing their student loans or combining many loans into one. Whatever the strategy, the secret to successful debt management is discipline and consistency, which guarantees on-time monthly payments and gradual debt reduction without impeding long-term financial objectives.

Last but not least, both financial security and personal development depend on upholding financial discipline. It can be tempting for people to spend more on non-essential products or lifestyle enhancements as they pay back their loans and advance in their careers.

Prioritizing financial discipline is crucial, though, if you want to genuinely accumulate wealth and succeed financially in the long run. Borrowers need to focus on investing, saving, and creating an emergency fund rather than giving in to the temptation to consume.

Borrowers can make sure that their educational investments continue to pay off in terms of both professional advancement and financial security by upholding a disciplined attitude to budgeting and financial management.

In conclusion, there are a lot of chances for both financial and personal development when borrowing strategically for schooling and professional development. People can use loans as a tool to open up new employment prospects and accumulate long-term wealth by carefully weighing the return on investment (ROI) of their education, managing their debt well, and striking a balance between payments and enhanced earning potential.

By implementing good debt management techniques, people may secure their future in a work market that is becoming more competitive and dynamic while still maintaining financial security and continuing to engage in their personal development.

Thought Room

What educational or skill-based opportunities are you willing to borrow for to advance your career?

How can you ensure that the investment in your education yields a return on your investment?

What are the long-term financial implications of borrowing for personal growth, and how can you prepare for them?

Chapter 4
Scaling Businesses with Debt Financing

"The way to get started is to quit talking and begin doing." — Walt Disney

The Role of Business Loans in Startup Growth

In the early phases of starting a business, entrepreneurs frequently encounter major obstacles. Getting enough money to pay for startup costs like inventory, equipment, marketing, and staffing is one of the biggest challenges. In order to close the gap between an entrepreneur's dream and the reality of creating a successful company, business loans are essential.

By taking out loans, entrepreneurs are able to raise the money they need to launch their businesses and focus on expansion rather than budgetary restraints. These loans enable firms to expand quickly without immediately depending on personal funds or outside investors, and they can cover a wide variety of costs.

Loans can offer a much-needed capital infusion to entrepreneurs in the early phases of business growth, assisting them in overcoming the initial financial obstacles. For instance, a loan enables the business owner to make expenditures without waiting for revenues if the company wants to buy equipment or find a location.

Additionally, loans can be used to pay for marketing expenses that support system development, hiring, and brand awareness. With this funding, companies can have the time they need to become well-known, attract clients, and begin making money before having to devote all of their attention to debt repayment. To put it simply, borrowing money can be a calculated tactic for financing and quickening the growth trajectory of a firm.

Small firms and startups can choose from a variety of credit options, each designed to meet their unique requirements and financial circumstances. Among the most popular options are traditional bank loans, which have comparatively low interest rates but call for thorough business plans and high credit scores.

Businesses with a proven track record and a distinct revenue model are the best candidates for these loans. As an alternative, entrepreneurs frequently use SBA (Small Business Administration) loans because they are backed by the government and typically have less stringent restrictions. For business owners who might not be eligible for conventional funding, microloans—

smaller loans sometimes provided by community lenders or nonprofit organizations—are an additional choice.

For firms that require flexibility in managing cash flow or meeting immediate financial demands, business credit cards, lines of credit, and invoice financing are also viable options. Entrepreneurs must be aware of the range of loan possibilities in order to select the best one for their company.

Debt finance has been used by many prosperous companies to expand their operations and achieve quick growth. Amazon is a good example. Jeff Bezos used loans and investments to finance the company's expansion in the early years, covering expenses for customer acquisition and infrastructure.

Bezos was able to grow his company before it turned a profit by taking on debt early on. Starbucks is another example of a company that has used business loans to expand its operations and increase brand awareness.

In both situations, the loans played a crucial role in assisting these businesses in getting to a place where they could make enough money to pay back the debt and continue operating for the long run. These success examples demonstrate the important part debt funding can play in a company's development, particularly when paired with a sound business plan and excellent execution.

Finding the Loan Repayment Break-Even Point

Any corporation that takes on debt must comprehend the break-even threshold. It is the moment at which all of a company's expenses, including both fixed and variable expenditures, are equal to its revenues. The break-even point is a crucial indicator for new businesses that depend on business loans since it shows when the company will start making enough money to pay off its debt.

Entrepreneurs can determine whether their company is on pace to repay loans while maintaining profitability by computing this point. Startups may manage their cash flow and set plans for future expansion by knowing how loan repayment fits into the larger financial picture.

Businesses must first comprehend the difference between fixed and variable costs in order to determine the break-even point. Rent, salary, and loan payments are examples of fixed costs—expenses that remain constant despite changes in business activity.

No matter how much money is made, these expenses never change and must be paid for. Conversely, variable expenses, including raw materials, shipping charges, or sales commissions, vary according to the volume of goods or services provided.

Businesses can calculate how much revenue is required to pay for both operating expenses and debt payments by combining these two cost categories. An essential technique for determining when a company can start turning a profit after paying its debts is the break-even analysis.

Businesses can begin estimating when they will break even after fixed and variable costs have been taken into consideration. The contribution margin, which is the difference between sales price and variable expenses, is divided by the total fixed costs to get the break-even threshold. This number aids business owners in calculating the amount of sales revenue needed to pay for operating costs and debt payback.

Since startups are frequently under pressure to expand rapidly while managing debt, reaching this break-even point is very crucial. Entrepreneurs can make plans and make sure they have enough cash flow to meet loan payback schedules by estimating when their business will achieve this milestone.

It is impossible to overestimate the significance of budgeting for debt payback during the scaling process. A company's financial responsibilities increase with its size. Entrepreneurs must carefully manage their money to prevent loan default because loan repayment schedules usually contain fixed payments that must be completed regardless of business performance. Budgeting guarantees that companies have sufficient cash on hand to pay for loans as well as operating expenses.

Furthermore, establishing a thorough financial plan that include loan payback schedules aids business owners in setting spending priorities, allocating funds sensibly, and preventing wasteful expenditure. A carefully considered budget also enables business managers to foresee financial difficulties, such varying revenue or unforeseen expenses, and modify their plans appropriately.

Keeping Your Finances in Check While Expanding Your Company

To ensure long-term success, scaling a business necessitates careful financial management. Entrepreneurs frequently have to strike a careful balance between paying off debt and making further investments in the expansion of their business.

Managing cash flow, or the flow of money into and out of the company, is one of the most important parts of this process. As businesses grow, they frequently need more funding to invest in marketing initiatives, recruit more employees, and pay for operating costs.

Businesses that have loans must simultaneously make sure they have adequate cash on hand to cover their debts. To maintain a healthy balance between meeting debt requirements and investing in growth, effective cash flow management entails monitoring income, expenses, and loan obligations.

Finding a balance between paying off debt and putting revenues back into the firm is crucial when expanding a company. When it comes to resource allocation, entrepreneurs may have to make tough choices between using money to build their business or rapidly pay off debt.

Reinvesting in the company may result in greater long-term growth, even while paying off debt fast can lower interest costs and increase financial stability. For example, increasing marketing efforts, creating new locations, or diversifying product lines can all result in new revenue streams that eventually boost the profitability of the company.

The secret is to evaluate each decision's return on investment (ROI) and give priority to spending that will yield the highest short- and long-term profits.

Using borrowed funds to scale has both risks and benefits. Leveraging debt can, on the one hand, give entrepreneurs the resources they need to expand their businesses rapidly and take advantage of market possibilities that might not otherwise be available. However, borrowing entails controlling the related financial risks and making sure that the loan is repaid on time.

A company may experience major repercussions, such as default, asset loss, or bankruptcy, if it is unable to make enough money to pay down its debt. But when properly handled, debt can be a potent instrument for raising market share, speeding up expansion, and raising the company's worth.

In order to maintain the financial stability of their company as it grows, entrepreneurs who scale using borrowed capital must continue to be strategic and disciplined in their management of both debt and growth.

To sum up, business loans are essential for startups to finance their early operations and successful expansion. Entrepreneurs can use borrowed cash to fuel growth without jeopardizing the viability of their firms by knowing the sorts of loans, figuring out the break-even point for debt repayment, and keeping their finances in check while expanding.

Strategic planning, careful debt management, and the capacity to decide when and how to reinvest in the business are all essential for success. When properly leveraged, business loans can transform a modest startup into a successful company and lay the groundwork for long-term success.

Thought Room

How would you approach taking on debt to scale your business without jeopardizing your financial health?

What key performance indicators (KPIs) will you use to measure the success of your debt-funded investments?

What are the potential risks of business loans, and how can you mitigate them?

Chapter 5
Maximizing Investments with Margin Loans

"The stock market is filled with individuals who know the price of everything, but the value of nothing." — *Philip Fisher*

How Margin Loans Work and Their Potential for Amplifying Returns

By leveraging their current investment portfolio as collateral, investors can increase their prospective profits through the utilization of margin loans. These loans increase an investor's purchasing power by enabling them to borrow funds from a brokerage to acquire more stocks.

Similar to a line of credit, this borrowing mechanism allows the investor to access a specific amount of money based on the value of the assets they currently possess. Margin loans don't compel the borrower to make set monthly payments like standard loans do. Rather, the investor must keep a minimum amount in their margin account (referred to as the margin requirement) and may be asked to pay back the loan at any point.

The use of securities as collateral is the primary characteristic that sets margin loans apart from other types of borrowing, including personal loans or mortgages. A piece of the investor's portfolio is pledged as collateral when they take out a margin loan, and the broker may liquidate this portion if the investor is unable to repay the loan.

An investor's borrowing capacity is usually expressed as a percentage of the value of their holdings, with an initial margin requirement that commonly falls between 50% and 70%.

For instance, if the margin requirement is 50% and an investor wants to purchase $10,000 worth of stocks, they would need to have $5,000 in equity in their account and may borrow the other $5,000 from the broker. By using this process, investors can increase their potential for profit by controlling a greater position with a smaller initial investment.

The ability of margin loans to increase investment portfolio returns is what makes them appealing. Investors who borrow money to buy more securities might profit from any rise in the value of those securities, increasing their profits in comparison to their original investment.

Because of the extra exposure from the borrowed funds, the return on the initial stock may exceed 10%, for instance, if the investor's portfolio appreciates by 10%. Margin loans are a powerful instrument for increasing profits in bull markets or times of rapid development because of the leverage effect, which enables investors to profit from higher gains in favorable market conditions. But there is also a higher chance of losing money along with the greater possibility for profit.

Margin loans put investors at higher risk even if they have the potential to yield sizable profits. Just as leverage can amplify benefits, it can also amplify losses. The investor's losses will be greater than their initial equity if the value of the securities they bought on margin declines.

In the worst situation, the investor can lose more than their original investment if the portfolio's value drops too much. Furthermore, brokers usually demand that investors have a maintenance margin—a minimum amount of equity in their margin accounts.

The investor may receive a margin call if the equity falls below this threshold due to a decline in the value of the securities, which would require them to sell some stocks or make additional deposits into the account in order to pay back the loan. Because investors must continuously check their portfolios to make sure they can meet these requirements, this creates a sense of urgency and risk.

Managing Risk in Margin Lending

Because of the potential for increased losses and the possibility of margin calls, margin lending carries a high risk. When the stocks in an investor's margin account lose value below the necessary maintenance margin, a margin call takes place. In order to lower the loan sum, the broker then requests that the investor either sell certain stocks or make more deposits into the account.

The broker may sell the securities in the account to cover the loan balance if the investor is unable to fulfill the margin call. Investors may find themselves in a situation where they must take immediate action, frequently in the face of adverse market conditions, as margin calls can occur without warning. For this reason, managing the risks involved with margin lending requires an understanding of margin calls.

Keeping an adequate cushion in the margin account is one of the key ways to defend against margin calls. Investors should try to maintain their equity far above the minimum criteria and refrain from taking out loans up to the maximum amount permitted by the broker.

This additional cushion lowers the chance of getting a margin call and acts as a buffer against market volatility. Investors should keep an eye on their portfolios and keep up with market developments in addition to keeping a good margin cushion. By doing this, they can foresee future declines and take preventative measures to avoid margin calls, such cutting back on their margin positions or selling off specific stocks.

For long-term success, a plan to reduce the risks associated with margin lending must be developed. Limiting the utilization of margin loans to a limited percentage of the whole portfolio is one popular tactic. Investors can reduce their risk exposure and steer clear of the large losses that might arise from excessive leverage by taking out cautious loans.

Stop-loss orders are another tool that investors should employ to automatically sell stocks if their price drops below a preset threshold. This can safeguard the investor's equity and reduce possible losses. Having a well-defined exit strategy is also crucial. The impact of adverse market movements might be lessened if an investor has a plan for when to reduce leverage or cut losses if the market moves against their position.

Another essential element of risk management while using margin loans is diversifying the investment portfolio. Investors can lessen their exposure to any one asset or market by distributing their assets over a number of asset classes, industries, and geographical areas.

Diversification makes ensuring that a decline in one part of the market does not have an outsized effect on the portfolio as a whole and helps to even over the volatility of individual assets. Furthermore, because the value of the holdings in a diversified portfolio is less likely to drop sharply overall, it is less likely to result in a margin call. The likelihood that an investor may experience large losses or have to sell holdings to satisfy margin needs decreases with portfolio diversity.

Utilizing Margin Loans to Create a Balanced Portfolio

Investors looking to manage risk and optimize returns may find that using margin loans to create a balanced portfolio works well. The opportunity to diversify investments across many asset classes, including stocks, bonds, commodities, and real estate, is a major benefit of margin loans.

Investors can increase the size of their portfolios beyond what their own capital would permit by borrowing money. More exposure to different markets, sectors, and investment opportunities is made possible by this, which could raise the portfolio's overall return.

Each asset class's risk profile should be taken into account while creating a balanced portfolio. For instance, bonds give more consistent returns at lower rates, but equities often have bigger potential returns but are more volatile. Investing across a variety of asset classes allows investors to take advantage of growth prospects while lowering the overall risk of their portfolio.

Additional securities, like stocks or real estate, can be bought with margin loans to increase the portfolio's overall return. Nonetheless, it is crucial to prevent overexposure to any one investment type and to be aware of the leverage involved. The purpose of a balanced portfolio should be to include a variety of assets that fit the investor's risk tolerance and financial objectives.

It takes rigorous preparation and self-control to use margin loans to create a long-term, risk-balanced portfolio. Investors should resist the urge to use high leverage in an attempt to pursue short-term gains, as this could result in large losses should the market go against them. Rather, concentrate on creating a portfolio that supports long-term goals and is built to withstand market swings.

To make sure that the asset allocation stays balanced and in accordance with the investor's objectives, regular portfolio assessments and adjustments are crucial. Additionally, investors should review their use of margin loans on a regular basis to make sure that their leverage is suitable for their risk tolerance and financial status.

Achieving significant investment returns while managing debt requires careful balancing. Margin loans must be utilized carefully, but they might give you the extra money you need to take advantage of investing opportunities. Significant financial pressure could result from over-leveraging if market conditions suddenly change.

Investors should avoid borrowing more than is permitted and concentrate on keeping a healthy amount of equity in their margin accounts in order to manage debt properly. Investors should also exercise discipline when it comes to margin loans and refrain from using borrowed money for short-term transactions or speculative investments. Investors can minimize borrowing risks and generate significant profits by carefully utilizing margin loans and constructing a long-term, diversified portfolio.

In summary, margin loans include a lot of risks but can be an effective way to increase returns. Investors can minimize the risks of over-leveraging while achieving their financial objectives by comprehending how margin loans operate, controlling the risks involved, and strategically utilizing them within a balanced portfolio.

Investors can efficiently use margin loans to increase their investment returns without taking on excessive risk provided they diversify their holdings, keep adequate equity, and periodically review their portfolios.

Thought Room

Do you understand the risks involved in using margin loans for investing, and how comfortable are you with them?

How can you balance leveraging debt with ensuring a safe, diversified investment strategy?

What is your plan for managing margin calls and avoiding excessive risk?

Chapter 6

Financing Passive Income Streams

"Don't work for money, make it work for you." — *Robert Kiyosaki*

Identifying Profitable Passive Income Opportunities

Entrepreneurs have many choices to consider when it comes to accumulating money through passive income. There are several types of passive income sources, including digital goods, real estate investments, and e-commerce. Over time, e-commerce has changed, and sites like Amazon, Etsy, and eBay now offer opportunities.

Entrepreneurs have the option of opening physical stores, dropshipping, or even selling digital products. For instance, dropshipping involves a supplier who sends goods straight to consumers, eliminating the need for the seller to manage inventory. With this strategy, business owners can turn a profit without having to pay the overhead expenses that come with running a conventional retail establishment.

Similarly, after the product is developed and promoted, selling digital goods like software, eBooks, or online courses can produce a steady flow of revenue. Digital products have enormous scalability since they may be duplicated without incurring extra production costs.

Another well-liked source of passive income is real estate. Purchasing rental properties can result in a consistent flow of income, which can be particularly profitable if the properties are located in locations with strong demand. Additionally, real estate has the possibility for appreciation, in which the property's value rises with time.

Even though it costs a lot of money up front, it can pay off handsomely. Another way to invest in commercial real estate without actually owning or managing properties is through real estate investment trusts, or REITs. Flipping homes or purchasing holiday rentals on websites like Airbnb have grown to be profitable options for short-term investors looking to make passive income.

The purchase of dividend-paying stocks or bonds is another noteworthy source of passive income. With this kind of investment, people can generate a consistent income by receiving regular distributions without having to sell their shares. Additionally, once they have an audience, content-based enterprises like blogs or YouTube channels can turn a profit. These platforms make money through sponsorships, affiliate marketing, and ad revenue. Every one of these passive income sources has pros and cons of its own, and choosing the best one relies on a number of variables, including the investor's risk tolerance, available funds, and skill set.

Passive income enterprises are particularly appealing because of their potential for growth. Many passive revenue streams can be expanded with little assistance from the entrepreneur once a business model has been established. For example, it is relatively inexpensive to promote a digital product, such as an online course, to a worldwide audience after it has been created.

On the other hand, real estate investments can produce passive income from a number of properties, and the potential for income rises with the number of properties. Scalability, however, is contingent upon the state of the market as well as the capacity of the individual to efficiently manage and grow their investments. Making sure the system can accommodate growing demand without requiring a corresponding rise in work or expense is the key to scalability.

Evaluating market demand and long-term sustainability is crucial for finding lucrative passive income prospects. An e-commerce site, for instance, may prosper at first but may experience market saturation or shifts in customer behavior.

Similar to this, real estate markets are subject to change, so before spending a lot of money, it's critical to think about a location's potential for future growth.

It is essential to comprehend long-term sustainability in order to steer clear of hazardous investments. Entrepreneurs should investigate consumer behavior, market trends, and the industry's stability before making an investment. They can guarantee the long-term profitability of the passive income potential by doing this.

Getting Funding for Projects That Generate Passive Income

One of the first challenges in launching a passive income business is frequently obtaining funding. Some people might need to hunt for loans to get started, while others could have the money to cover their initial investments.

Small loans can supply the start-up money required for passive income streams, including financing the development of a digital product, the acquisition of real estate, or the purchase of e-commerce inventory.

Although internet lenders and traditional bank loans are popular choices, business owners should carefully review the loan's terms, such as interest rates and repayment plans, to make sure they can manage the debt while making money.

Loans can be used to finance the establishment of a digital storefront or to buy products in bulk when it comes to funding inventory for an e-commerce company. A small loan, for instance, can enable an entrepreneur to engage in website development and marketing or purchase a stock of goods to offer in their online store.

Small loans can also be used to finance the down payment for investment properties, like vacation rentals or rental homes, in the real estate market. A strong credit score and a thorough business plan that details how the loan will be paid back through passive revenue may be necessary to secure funding for these endeavors.

Loans for software development or marketing initiatives to increase visitors to online stores may be necessary for companies that are primarily focused on technology or automated processes. By investing in customer relationship management (CRM) systems, developing automation tools, or launching paid advertising campaigns, entrepreneurs can use loans to expand their company's infrastructure.

By obtaining funding for these essential components, the business owner is putting himself in a position to grow faster and more effectively, guaranteeing that the passive revenue flow will eventually pay off the loan balance and keep making money.

For entrepreneurs who generate passive income, it is essential to investigate several financing possibilities because they can differ significantly in terms of eligibility and cost. Entrepreneurs can think about small business loans, peer-to-peer lending, or even credit lines in addition to conventional bank loans. Every one of these financing choices has pros and cons of its own.

Peer-to-peer lending services, for instance, frequently offer quicker access to capital, but they could also have higher interest rates. Conversely, a line of credit allows for flexibility and only demands repayment for the amount that is drawn. Entrepreneurs can make well-informed selections that support their financial objectives by closely weighing their options and comprehending the terms.

Automating and Growing Your Passive Income for Long-Term Achievement

For long-term success, scaling and automating a passive income stream is the next step after it has been developed. Converting a side project into a completely automated revenue stream entails developing mechanisms that, once established, require little maintenance. By connecting third-party platforms, for instance, an e-commerce company can automate order fulfillment, inventory management, and customer support. Setting up an online platform where clients can buy and download digital products without requiring manual intervention is the key to automation.

Simplifying operations is an essential part of growing a passive income business. An entrepreneur can save time and effort by automating more of their business. Email marketing campaigns, for instance, can be planned ahead of time and configured to send on autopilot. Automated billing and delivery systems can be used by subscription-based organizations, such as digital content subscriptions or membership websites.

A totally passive business model can be developed by entrepreneurs by utilizing technology and outsourcing work wherever feasible. The objective is to create procedures that function without continual input so that the company may make money while the entrepreneur concentrates on other endeavors.

In order to ensure long-term sustainability, strategies for managing passive income systems with the least amount of personal engagement are essential. Investing in systems that automatically track and modify the performance of the company is one strategy.

For instance, an entrepreneur can make data-driven decisions without actively managing daily operations by employing analytics tools to monitor sales, customer behavior, and website traffic. Additionally, outsourcing customer support or hiring virtual assistants might provide business owners more time to concentrate on strategy and expansion.

One important tactic for building long-term wealth is reinvesting passive income profits to create new streams. Entrepreneurs can take the gains and put them back into other projects once the original passive income source is consistently bringing in money.

Profits from a profitable e-commerce venture, for example, could be utilized to finance the development of new digital goods or real estate investments. Reinvesting revenue allows the entrepreneur to diversify their sources of income and increase their wealth over time, protecting them from the hazards that come with depending solely on one passive income source.

In summary, automating and growing passive income for long-term success is a slow process that calls for strategic execution and meticulous planning. Entrepreneurs can create companies that need little continuous work while yielding significant returns by utilizing technology, outsourcing work, and reinvesting earnings into new revenue streams.

Passive income projects have the potential to develop into a long-term, sustainable means of accumulating wealth if the proper framework is in place.

Thought Room

What passive income stream could you start today, and how can debt financing play a role in your growth?

Are you willing to reinvest the income generated by passive ventures to scale them further?

How can you ensure the sustainability of your passive income streams while minimizing risk?

Conclusion

To sum up, The Borrower's Advantage: Turning Loans Into Wealth offers a strong foundation for using borrowing to boost financial and personal development.

We have discussed in this book how loans, when utilized wisely, can enable investors, entrepreneurs, and individuals to seize opportunities and create lasting wealth. Understanding how borrowing may be used efficiently in a variety of contexts—from real estate and education to business expansion and passive income—is essential to this approach.

This book's main idea is very clear: when handled properly, debt may increase wealth and create possibilities rather than being a burden. But as we covered in each chapter, this tactic calls for understanding, self-control, and a readiness to take measured chances. It's about learning how to use debt to generate leverage and unlock higher financial returns, not about avoiding it.

Chapter 1: Building Wealth Through Real Estate Financing emphasized that real estate is one of the most reliable ways to build wealth, and leveraging mortgages allows you to control larger properties with less capital upfront. Through strategic investments, you can amplify your returns and build a sustainable income stream. The key takeaway here is that, just like the Chinese proverb suggests, the best time to start investing was 20 years ago, but the second-best time is now.

Chapter 2: The Power of Borrowing for Personal Growth highlighted the importance of borrowing for education and personal development. By using loans to invest in your skills, you increase your earning potential, opening up opportunities for career advancement and long-term financial success. This chapter drives home the value of investing in yourself—an investment that will pay off multiple times over.

Chapter 3: Scaling Businesses with Debt Financing explored how borrowing can be the fuel that drives business expansion. Whether you're just starting or looking to scale, loans can give your business the financial support it needs to grow. The chapter emphasized the importance of calculating risks and returns, and balancing debt servicing with reinvestment to ensure long-term sustainability.

Chapter 4: Maximizing Investments with Margin Loans explained how margin loans can be used to enhance your investment portfolio. While margin loans offer the potential for substantial returns, they come with inherent risks. The key is to balance leverage with a diversified portfolio, reducing your exposure to volatility while maximizing your growth potential.

Chapter 5: Financing Passive Income Streams examined how debt can be used to fuel the creation of scalable passive income streams. By securing financing for ventures like real estate, e-commerce, or digital products, you can generate long-term, automated income without constantly working for every dollar.

This chapter stressed the importance of reinvesting earnings to build even more passive income streams, ultimately leading to financial independence.

In each of these chapters, the idea that borrowing is a tool to build wealth and increase financial opportunities has been reinforced. Whether you're investing in real estate, growing a business, or financing your education, loans can give you the leverage to achieve your financial goals. However, it's vital to approach borrowing with caution, knowledge, and a plan for managing debt responsibly.

To summarize the key lessons from this book:

- In **Chapter 1**, you learned how leveraging mortgages can help you acquire real estate and build wealth over time.

- **Chapter 2** taught you how borrowing for education can increase your earning potential and advance your career.

- **Chapter 3** showed you how business loans can fuel your company's growth, and how to calculate when you'll break even and start profiting.

- **Chapter 4** highlighted how margin loans can amplify investment returns, while also teaching you how to mitigate risks with a diversified portfolio.

- **Chapter 5** discussed how debt can be used to finance passive income streams that provide financial freedom over time.

Now that you have a clearer understanding of how borrowing can work to your advantage, it's time to take action. You have the tools, the knowledge, and the strategies necessary to start using loans to create wealth. Whether it's buying your first investment property, pursuing further education, or scaling your business, the power is in your hands to make debt work for you.

Don't let fear or uncertainty hold you back from seizing these opportunities. Remember, the earlier you begin, the greater the rewards. Take the leap today and start implementing the strategies you've learned in this book. Whether you choose to borrow for education, investment, or business growth, make sure to do so with a clear plan in place.

Start by assessing your financial situation, identifying where you can leverage debt responsibly, and creating a roadmap for your wealth-building journey. The world is full of opportunities—take advantage of them, and transform your financial future today. Your path to wealth and financial freedom starts now.

www.ingramcontent.com/pod-product-compliance
Lightning Source LLC
Chambersburg PA
CBHW070342230526
45471CB00006B/2419